# A TRANSCULTURAL MOSAIC

SELECTIONS FROM THE PERMANENT COLLECTION OF MINGEI INTERNATIONAL / MUSEUM OF WORLD FOLK ART

DESIGNED AND EDITED BY MARTHA W. LONGENECKER

PHOTOGRAPHY BY LYNTON GARDINER     (except as noted)

Library of Congress Catalog No. 89-50416
Published by Mingei International
Museum of World Folk Art

University Towne Centre, 4405 La Jolla Village Drive,
San Diego, CA 92122
(mailing address: P. O. Box 553, La Jolla, CA 92038)

Copyright © 1993
by Mingei International Museum

# A MINGEI INTERNATIONAL MUSEUM DOCUMENTARY PUBLICATION
MADE POSSIBLE BY THE SEYMOUR E. CLONICK AND SYDNEY MARTIN ROTH PUBLICATION FUND

ADDITIONAL FUNDING FROM THE JOSEPH DROWN FOUNDATION AND NORA AND ALAN JAFFE

DEDICATION AND ACKNOWLEDGMENTS

**ALL WHO ARE A PART OF THE EVER-EVOLVING CYCLE OF ART**

**THE CREATORS** who sensitively and skillfully transform the natural materials of their environment into useful, beautiful objects — so essential to our daily lives.

**THE COLLECTORS** who cherish and care for these arts, serving as trustees through whose hands they pass for others to enjoy.

**THE DONORS** to MINGEI INTERNATIONAL MUSEUM'S permanent collection and all who contribute to the continuing creation of the museum — a living place where arts of the people (mingei) speak for themselves in the international language of art that knows no barriers of time, place or culture. Revealing the distinctions and similarity of individuals and cultures, their creative power inspires new expression — the cycle of art is completed to begin anew.

# CONTENTS

## Introduction by Martha W. Longenecker

"A picture is worth a thousand words," and this is a picture-book of arts created by people from many times and places throughout the world. It invites you to look and see, reading the visual language of line, form and color. The pictures acquaint you with selections from MINGEI INTERNATIONAL—Museum of World Folk Art's permanent collection — ninety pieces from over five thousand.

This book also invites you to come to MINGEI INTERNATIONAL MUSEUM and see the real objects — the *seeing* of which is worth *countless* words.

These are useful arts that are satisfying to the human spirit. Made by hand, they are created from common and readily available materials of our earth — clay, wood, fiber, metal, stone, bone, shell, pigment and other natural substances. Their value is not in the intrinsic worth of the material — as in the case of jewelry made of precious metals and stones — but in the unique, expressive way their creators transcend materials and techniques with honest expressions of enduring value.

The arts of the people are simple and unassuming. Easily understood, they do not burden us psychologically. Although they may inspire intellectual curiosity — fulfilled through reading and research — the joy in seeing and using these arts is not dependent on knowledge.

*Mingei is a special transcultural word meaning "arts of the people" combining the Japanese words for people (min) and art (gei).*

It was coined in the early part of the twentieth century by the late Dr. Soetsu Yanagi, revered and visionary scholar of Japan. As a visiting professor lecturing on Japanese art history at Harvard University from September 1929 to August 1930, he observed that many articles made by unknown craftsmen of pre-industrialized times were of a beauty seldom equaled by artists of modern societies. He questioned why this might be, until he gained insight regarding the nature of things which are integrally related to life — and born of a state of mind not attached to a conscious idea of beauty or ugliness. He recognized that unsurpassed beauty was the flowering of a unified expression when there is no division of head, heart and hands. He further realized that in the contemporary world of increasing mechanization and fragmentation of activities, more and more people seldom perform an act of total attention. During the early industrialization of Japan he awakened people to the essential need to continue making and using handmade objects which express the whole being — body, mind and spirit.

To communicate this profound insight, Dr. Yanagi, together with the potters Shoji Hamada and Kanjiro Kawai, founded the Mingei Association and in 1936 established in Tokyo the first Folk Art Museum in Japan. A second museum in the city of Kurashiki, was founded by K. Tonomoura in 1948. As the meaning of of the word mingei was increasingly understood, other museums followed. Living art traditions of Japan that have endured unbroken for thousands of years were not lost to present and future generations as is happening throughout much of the industrialized world.

Dr. Yanagi's inspiring teachings maintain that creative, aesthetic capacity is normal and natural for all people and that it was only in abnormal, degenerate times that people were singled out as so-called geniuses and artists by the masses who were not actualizing their own innate creative power.

Illustrating his point he said, "Let us suppose that I speak English exceedingly well. All my Japanese friends would say, 'He is very good in English,' I should be a genius as far as English goes, a hero and an artist of language. But let us remember that, however excellent my command of English may be, I should be a poor English speaker compared to native Englishmen. On the other hand, all Englishmen are born good, we might say, especially talented, in the language. In England even a fool may speak English fluently, and dogs understand spoken English. However good an Englishman may be in speaking English he is not given recognition for that alone. Rather, it is quite usual to speak English well, because all Englishmen speak English. However good he may be, he is not considered a genius. In other words, all Englishmen are only artisans as far as speaking English is concerned. But if they should suddenly become as poor as the Japanese in speaking English, then some few of them would be singled out as artists. But these artists are likely to speak no more proper English than they did when they were mere artisans, that is, before their friends lost command of the language."*

Many of the contemporary craftsmen who were nurtured by Yanagi's teaching became "Living National Treasures of Japan," and their work possesses qualities of naturalness and beauty akin to that of the unknown craftsmen of prior days. The stencil dye designs by Keisuke Serizawa are notable examples.

The world-renowned wood block artist, Shiko Munakata, emphatically proclaimed "I'm not a genius — just a remnant!"

My introduction to these liberating teachings was a turning point in my life. It happened while I was still a university student when my mother's Christmas gift made it possible for me to attend the December 1952 Potter's Seminar in Los Angeles with Dr. Yanagi,

*from *Folk Arts of Japan* by Soetsu Yanagi

Shoji Hamada and the English potter and author, Bernard Leach. His books, *The Potter's Book, Hamada,* and adaptation of Soetsu Yanagi's writings, *The Unknown Craftsman* convey the world significance of mingei, as did these craftsmen's seminars.

Although these teachers urged me to come to Japan immediately, it was ten years before I was able to accept their kind invitation. Through the friendship and assistance of Dr. Yanagi's cousin, Tsune Sesoko, I was prepared for my future journey.

The opportunity came in 1962, when as a professor of art, teaching ceramics at San Diego State University, I was awarded a sabbatical leave to go to Japan. Studying under the guidance of Shoji Hamada and working at his kiln and that of Tatsuzo Shimoaka in the city of Mashiko, I came to see the close relationship between daily life and work.

In the following years, Mr. Hamada and Mr. Shimoaka responded to our invitations and visited the United States to lecture, exhibit and demonstrate pottery making. As I returned again and again for further study in Japan, it became clear that an organization was necessary to facilitate these cultural exchanges.

With the encouragement of my late husband, Sydney Martin Roth, who provided the seed money for incorporation in 1974, MINGEI INTERNATIONAL became a nonprofit, public foundation dedicated to furthering the understanding of "arts of people" (mingei) from all cultures of the world.

In 1978, with an idea initiated by Judy Munk, and an unprecedented gift of a twenty-year leasehold provided by University Towne Centre and Ernest W. Hahn and Associates, the members of MINGEI INTERNATIONAL designed and built its first museum. Now in its sixteenth year, fifty-one dynamic, changing exhibitions have been organized and presented — several of which have travelled throughout the United States. Supplemented by an audio/visual folk art reference library, these exhibitions are enriched by an active educational program including related illustrated lectures, films, music and dance. Their influence is extended by documentary exhibition publications distributed throughout the world.

To accommodate its expanding collections and museum program, the members of MINGEI INTERNATIONAL look forward to building *the museum of the future* — a permanent facility opening a broad yet intimate view of our magnificent world — A TRANSCULTURAL MOSAIC of timeless arts of the people.

*Martha W. Longenecker, founder/director of MINGEI INTERNATIONAL MUSEUM.*

**An Excerpt from *The Way of Tea*, a writing by Dr. Soetsu Yanagi**

They say; before all else, they saw. They were able to see. Ancient mysteries flow out of this spring of seeing.

Everyone sees things. But all people do not see them in the same manner; therefore, they do not perceive the same thing. Some may see into the depth of things, others see only the surface; and the objects seen may be divided into right and wrong. To see and misapprehend is but little better than not to notice. Though everyone says he sees things, how few can see things properly. Among these few are found our early masters of *Cha-no-yu* (we will call them Tea-Masters). They could comprehend intuitively. And because of their penetration, they saw truth.

What was their way of seeing? They saw *directly.* This directness makes all the difference in the world. It is a wonderful experience to attain the object directly through the eye. Most people look through some medium, generally inserting something between the eye and the object. Some interpose their thoughts or their personal tastes, others their habits. Assuredly these stimulate different points of view; but it is quite another thing to see directly. Seeing directly constitutes a direct communion between the eye and the object. Unless we see a thing without mediation, we cannot grasp the thing itself. The eminent Tea Masters were capable of this directness, a capacity which is, indeed, the test of genuine Tea Mastership. Only the masters who can do this are true Men of Tea, just as those who can see God face to face are the real priests worthy of the name. *Men of Tea* are masters of the power of seeing.

What, then, did the Tea Masters see face-to-face? What did their seeing eyes disclose? It was the reflection of the inner nature of things. Or, we might say, it was the seeing of the reality of things, which the old philosophers used to call "the eternal mode." It is not seeing a part of the thing, but the thing itself. The whole is not the sum total of the parts. The sum total and the whole are two distinct things. The whole is indivisible; it cannot be divided. To see the whole directly means to see before thinking, with no time for discrimination. If we look at things with our thoughts, we see only a portion; if we use our intellect before we see, our understanding will be superficial. We learn more through the power of seeing than through the power of intellectual understanding. There is a passage in a religious book which reads: "He who would know before he believeth cometh never to the true knowledge of God." It is the same with the beautiful. These who employ their intellect before they see are denied a real comprehension of beauty. Before all else the devotees of Tea saw. They applied their eyes directly to the objects.

## Commentary by Robert Bruce Inverarity

*on A TRANSCULTURAL MOSAIC—which was the premier exhibition of selections from the permanent collection of Mingei International and the inspiration for this publication.*

It can be a startling experience for many people to walk suddenly into a museum or gallery filled with cases containing unfamiliar objects and walls hung with odd-shaped pieces of wood or textiles. Certainly, if you have not been a regular or even an occasional museum visitor, or have been concerned only with drawings, interiors, furniture and paintings, such an exhibition will intrigue you more than you might imagine. As you quickly glance about, you may discover a familiar form, perhaps a doll, and thus form an immediate relationship with and interest in other objects on exhibition.

You might wonder what this is all about? The name, MINGEI INTERNATIONAL — Museum of World Folk Art, gives you a clue, but what is folk art? The answer to this question is not easy to give since experts in the field vary in their interpretation.

However, certain things are clear. Folk art is often thought of as popular art, including objects of practical use and wear. It is generally based on traditional forms produced by and for the people, with techniques and variations handed down from one generation to another.

A Hungarian woman embroidering an apron, or a New Mexican santero carving a figure for his church are folk artists producing objects which in form and type are traditional to the region and the people who make them. The environment and the fact that materials used are generally those available within a given area frequently affect the form of the finished object. A Greenland parka and a New Zealand flax cape are widely different in appearance, but both are articles of clothing made from available materials, suited to the climate in which each is worn and to the tastes of the people who wear them.

Some objects, such as handmade laces or fine jewelry, which also appeal to sophisticated taste, may be made for the majority of the people in the culture that produces them and thus are considered folk art. Many mass-produced handmade objects, such as Mexican pottery, are also classified as folk art since they are traditional forms produced by hand for the people of the culture.

What is the meaning in all this? Although the use of these practical items is usually self evident — a chair is a chair, a doll a doll — sometimes the object's meaning is not obvious because it embodies a spiritual element, as in African sculpture.

This exhibition at MINGEI INTERNATIONAL MUSEUM is an extraordinary display of superb examples of folk art from places many of us have not been to and from others that are unknown to us. The appealing diversity of this collection represents but the tip of an iceberg. Here over two hundred objects have been carefully selected from the Museum's collection of over five thousand items, it is truly a collector's collection. Each piece has been chosen with great taste and concern to afford the rare opportunity of a unique experience. Here you are able to see some of the finest examples of "art of the people."

Truly, this is a wonderful journey around the world — the miniature facade of an Indian temple, an Austrian hope chest copius enough to contain a groom, a shawl from Romania, an African granary door, an illustrated manuscript from Ethiopia, wonderful life-sized terra cotta animals made at the Museum in 1984 by artists/ craftsmen who came from India specifically to create them, a three foot tall terra cotta figure by Teodora Blanco of Oaxaca, Mexico. Textiles and pots from Middle and South America, a puppet from Thailand as realistic as the duck it represents...yes, all this and much more is beautifully displayed, well-lit and clearly labeled.

A TRANSCULTURAL MOSAIC is an exceptional, important and most successful exhibition — a great credit to the staff — an artistic triumph itself. Oh yes, I hope you see one of my favorites — a tiny Eskimo doll made of bone — it still hangs in my memory.

*Robert Bruce Inverarity, author, scholar and a foremost collector of northwest American Indian art, was the founding director for The International Folk Art Museum in Santa Fe, New Mexico. As a professional museum consultant, he has served on Mingei International's Advisory Board since the founding of this museum in 1978.*

CALLIGRAPHY
Soetsu Yanagi
over background Chinese Character by
Keisuke Serizawa

An approximate interpretation of the calligraphy is
"first of all — just six letters" referring to the
Buddhist phrase, Na-Mu-A-Mi-Da-Butsu, which
may be translated as "yield your will to the
Buddha." (Not a deity, the Buddha is an
embodiment of enlightenment.)
ink on handmade paper   12" x 18"
Tokyo, Japan, 1960

Promised gift.

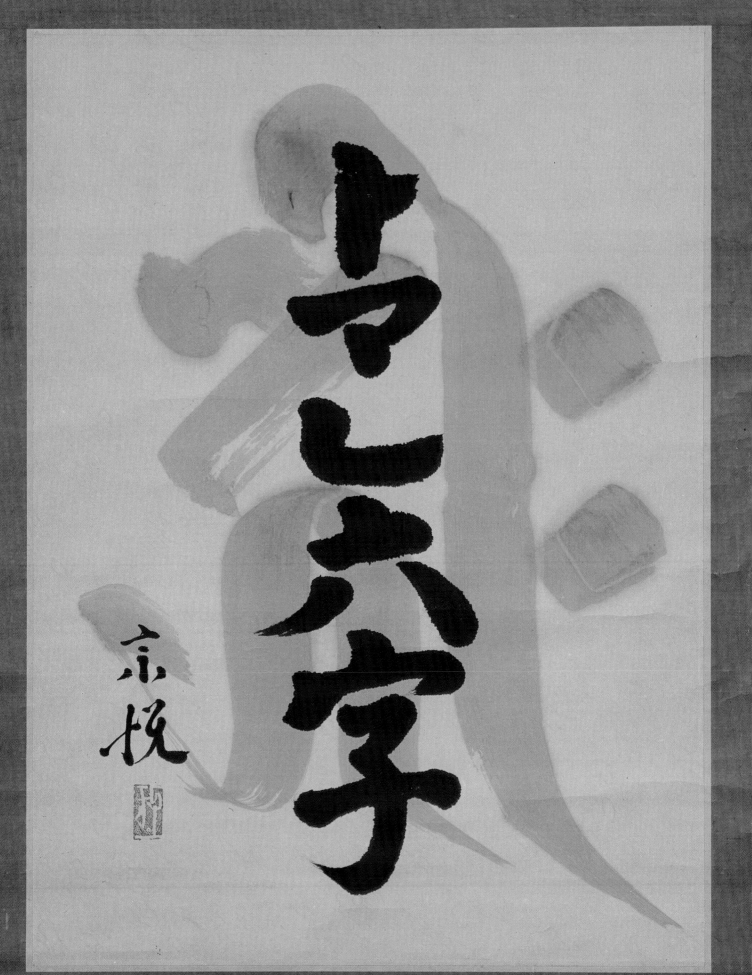

SQUARE BOTTLE
Shoji Hamada

Glazed stoneware   4" x 9"
Mashiko, Japan, 1965

14   Gift of Mr. and Mrs. Peter O'Reilly

WATER DROPPER
Shoji Hamada

glazed stoneware,   3" w.
Mashiko, Japan 1975

     Gift of Henry Huglin

BOTTLE
Kanjiro Kawai

glazed stoneware, 10½" h.
Kyoto, Japan 1942

Gift of Millard and Mary Sheets

BOWL
Tatsuzo Shimaoka

Glazed stoneware   20" d.
Japan, 1963

20   Gift of Mr. and Mrs. Robert Kinsey

BOWL
Arihiko Natsume

Lacquered wood   14" d.
Japan, 20th C

Gift of Arihiko Natsume

23

AINU COATS

cotton applique on plant fiber
Japan 19th C

Gift of Keisuke Serisawa

Photograph by Ann M. Kappes

AINU NECKLACE

Glass    36"
Hokkaido, Japan, 19th C

Gift of Keisuke Serizawa

CHEST

Wood and iron   8" x 13" x 10"
Japan, 19th C

Museum Purchase

TEXTILE

Cotton   32" x 36"
Okinawa, 20th C

Gift of Keisuke Serizawa

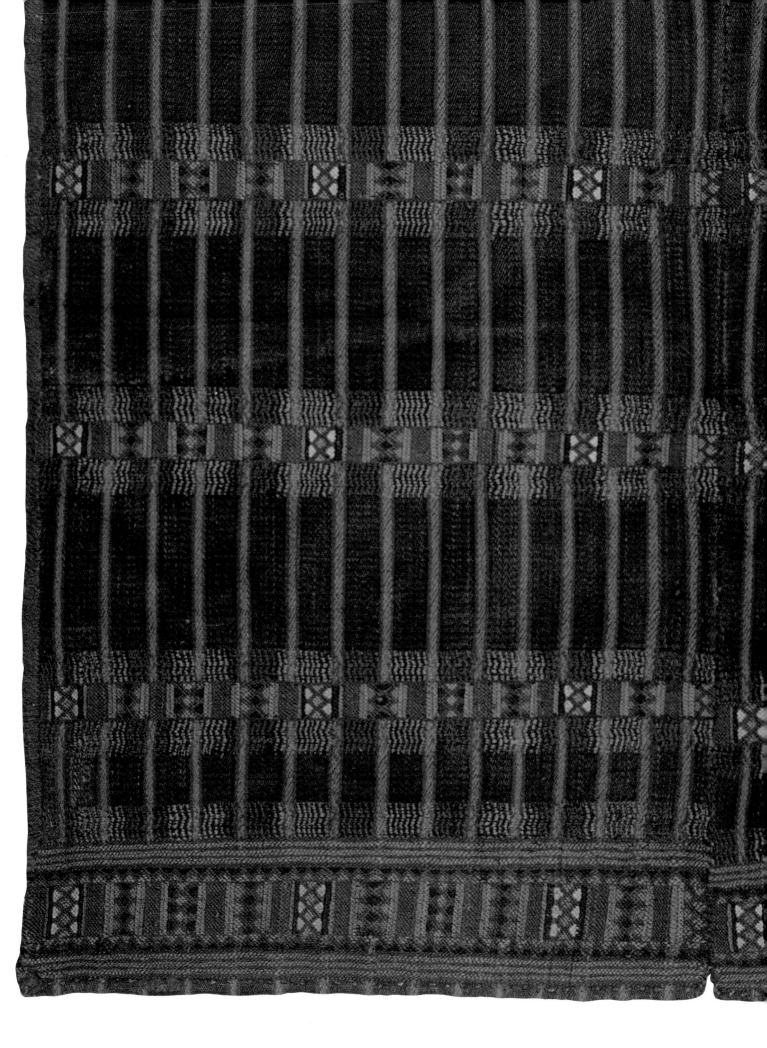

KOKESHI DOLL

Wood   7" x 24"
Japan, 19th C

   Gift of Fred and Barbara Meiers

32

*previous page*

## "DEATH OF BUDDHA"

Painting on paper   4' x 8'
Japan, early 18th C

Gift of Mr. John Boehme

## WATER DROPPER

Ceramic   3" d.
Korea, Yi Dynasty (1392–1910)

Gift of Edwin T. Harte

CHEST

Wood   38" x 18" x 45"
Korea, 19th C

DANCE MASK

Papier mache   10" x 15"
Korea, 20th C

Gift of the Korean Cultural Center, Los Angeles

CORNICE

Wood   16" x 7"
China, 19th C

Gift of Dr. and Mrs. Robert Buffum


BURIAL GARMENT

Painted paper   36" x 54"
China, 20th C

Gift of Florence Temko

SINGLE SLEEVE PANEL     HEADDRESS

silk embroidery 3" x 6"     silver 6" x 11"
Guizhou, China     Guizhou, China

     Gift of Peter Nelson     Museum purchase

COURT ROBE WITH SKIRT

Embroidered silk   24" x 55"
China, 19th C

44       Gift of Nancy Fitzwilliams

BOTTLE
Tze-chou Ware

glazed earthenware, 16" h.
China, Chin Dynasty 12th C

46    Gift of Mildred and Mary Sheets

CARPET DETAIL

handwoven wool 106" x 42"
Chinese-Tibetan border

Gift of Dr. and Mrs. Stanford Penner

PUPPET

Wood   13" x 10"
Thailand, 20th C

Museum Purchase

SHADOW PUPPET

Hide   48" x 58"
Thailand, 19th C

Gift of Ruth Shephard

RAMAYANA MASK,
Character of Lakshmana

wood, leather
Bali, Indonesia 20th C

Gift of Edward Inskeep

BEADED SKIRT

Indonesia, embroidery on cotton

Gift of Edward Inskeep

57

TEXTILE

embroidered cotton
Indonesia, 20th C

Gift of Edward Inskeep

TEXTILE

cotton Ikat
Indonesia, 20th C

Gift of Edward Inskeep

MASK OF GANESHA

Papier mache   8" x 15"
India, 20th C

Gift of Beatrice Wood

KRISHNA AS NATHAJI
Pichwai temple painting

cotton 81" x 94"
India, early 19th C

Gift of Martha Longenecker

MITHILA WALL PLAQUE

painted papier mache, 52" h.
Bihar, India, 1978

Gift of the Smithsonian Institution – Festival of India

PLATTER

Papier mache   18" d.
Kashmir, Srinagar, India, 1970

Gift of Mr. and Mrs. Anthony Browne

## KUTCH WOMAN'S BLOUSE

Embroidered, mirrored cotton    20" x 37"
Gujarat, India, 1978

Gift of Dr. and Mrs. Jonathan Fielding


*following page*

## CAST FIGURE

Brass    2" x 4"
India, 20th C

Gift of Louisa Kassler


## SAREE FRAGMENT

Silk ikat    7" x 14"
Pochampalli, India, 1973

Gift of Althea Lucic

WOMAN'S MARRIAGE SHAWL

Embroidered cotton   40" x 95"
Hazara, India, 20th C

Gift of Mr. and Mrs. Frederick Krieger

PATOLA SARI

Silk Ikat, 208" x 47"
Patan, India mid 20th C

Museum purchase

*previous page, left*

AIYNAR HORSE
by potter and priest, Palaniappan from India

Clay 6' h.
made at Mingei International Museum and fired at
Hazard Brick, during FORMS OF MOTHER EARTH,
a Festival of India exhibition, 1986.

*previous page, right*

AIYANAR HORSE
by potter and priest, Veeilan Sambandam from
India

clay   9' h.
made at Mingei International Museum and fired at
Hazard Brick, during exhibition The Horse in Folk
Art, 1984.

AIYANAR ELEPHANT
by potter and priest, Palaniappan from India

Clay 3' h.
made at Mingei International Museum and fired at
Hazard Brick, during FORMS OF MOTHER EARTH,
a Festival of India exhibition, 1986.

*following page*

"PABUJU KA PATA"
Backdrop painting for dancers, musicians and
story tellers

Gouache on handloomed cotton   280" x 67"
Udaipur, Rajasthan, India, c. 1870

Gift of Mr. and Mrs. Millard Sheets

NECKLACE

Silver   7" x 7"
Chitral, Pakistan, 20th C

84      Gift of Dr. Ronald Goldenson, M.D.

WOMAN'S HOOD

Textile with snow leopard teeth   8" x 25"
Pakistan, 1950

Gift of Mr. and Mrs. Christopher Well

SHAWL

Tie dyed silk   33" x 117"
Yazel, Iran, 20th C

Gift of the Estate of Tonia Gale

TEXTILE

painted and block-printed cotton 11" x 13"
Afghanistan

Museum purchase


*following page*

TEXTILE

handwoven wool   11' x 2½'
Syria 20th C

Gift of Lydia Yancy

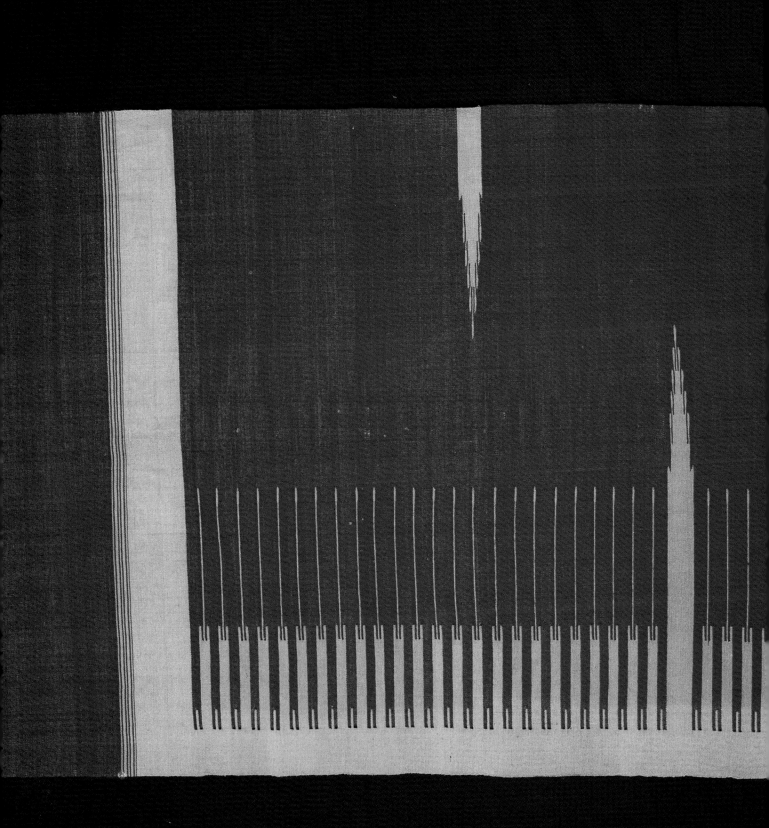

## WEDDING DRESS

silk embroidery on velvet, cotton and silk panels
Bethlehem, Palestine 1900

 Gift of Committee for the Preservation of Palestinian Heritage

SAB' ARWAH
(Seven Lives Necklace)

Silver   18"
Bethlehem, Palestine 1900


SHATWEH
(headcover)

silver, coins, coral, embroidery and applique
16" x 3½"
Bethlehem, Palestine 1900

Gift of Committee for the Preservation of Palestinian Heritage


SHAWL

Silk   23" x 130"
Romania, early 20th C

Gift of Louise Padelford

BLOUSE

white linen, beadwork, embroidery 20th C
Costisa, Romania

Gift of Paul and Ester Davis

BAUERNKASTEN (hope chest)

Wood   51" x 74"
Wald-in-Pinzgau, Austria, 1850

Gift of Dr. and Mrs. Arthur Metcalfe

BOWLS AND SERVING SPOON

Painted wood   3" to 6"
USSR, 1989

Gift of Martha Longenecker

PYZANKA
Ukrainian Easter Egg

Painted egg shell
USSR 1989


FESTIVAL FIGURE

Cheese   7" x 5"
USSR, 1989

104      Gift of Ludmira Uritskaya

TETE JUMEAU
Musical automated dolls

ceramic and mixed media   24" h.
France, 1860

106    Gift of Louise Padelford

APRON

Wool   31" x 25"
Portugal, 20th C

108       Gift of Louise Padelford

CHURCH FIGURE
of the Christ Child in Majesty

wood   22" h.
Spain, late 16th/early 17th C

110   Gift of Dorothy Dixon and Winnie Langley

ILLUSTRATED MANUSCRIPT

Parchment   3" x 4"
Ethiopia, 20th C

Gift of Mr. and Mrs. Robert Baumberger


MILK JUG

Calabash with cowrie shells   5" x 7"
Ethiopia, 20th C

Gift of Mr. and Mrs. Robert Baumberger

NECKLACE

bead and silver alloy    14" l.
Morocco, 20th C

Gift of Martha Longenecker

*previous page*

KABEJA
Hemba Janiform figure, "Kabeja"

Wood   4" x 11"
Eastern Zaire, Africa

Gift of Bernard Smolin
in Memory of Mims Smolin


BANMANA DOOR LOCK

Toro wood   15" x 14"
Mali, Africa

Gift of Bernard Smolin
in Memory of Mims Smolin

COMB

wood   10" h.
Africa, 20th C

Gift of Bernard Smolin

PORTABLE CHAIR

Wood   14" x 34"
Zaire, Africa, 20th C

 Gift of Mr. and Mrs. Horton Telford

DOGAN GRANARY DOOR

wood   4' h.
Mali, Africa, 20th C

124    Gift of Mr. and Mrs. Edmund Burke, The Frank Papworth Estate

SALAMPASU MASK

Mufuampo fiber   8" x 26"
Southern Zaire, Africa, 20th C

126     Gift of Mr. and Mrs. Horton Telford

## MWAASH-A-MBOY HELMET MASK

wicker, Kuba cloth, raffia, beads, coweries and
leather   23" h.
Zaire, 20th C

Gift of Mr and Mrs. George F. Wick

SCULPTURE

Metal   12" x 24"
Haiti, 20th C

Gift of the Estate of Clare Jordan

*previous page*

## CHIMU POT

Clay   5" x 7"
Peru

Gift of the Estate of Clare Jordan


*previous page*

## MANTA

Wool   42" x 47"
La Paz, Boliva, 20th C

Museum Purchase


## PRECOLUMBIAN TEXTILE FRAGMENT

Wool   12" x 15"
Peru

Gift of Hunton and Priscilla Sellman

BAG

Wool    13" x 13"
Guatemala, 20th C

Museum Purchase

*following page*

COLA
Tail panel of costume worn in
Corpus Christi Festival

Embroidered satin    21" x 45"
Ecuador, 20th C

Gift of Olga Fisch

*following page*

COLA
Tail panel of costume worn in
Corpus Christi Festival

Embroidered satin    23" x 47"
Ecuador, 20th C

Gift of Olga Fisch

CAROUSEL HORSE

Wood   25" x 20"
Mexico, 20th C

Gift of Marge Swenson

CLAY FIGURE
Teodora Blanco

terracotta, 37" h.
Oaxaca, Mexico, 20th C

    Gift of Fred and Barbara Meiers

## ANASAZI POT

Earthenware clay   3" x 5"
Four Corners Area, Arizona, USA, c. 700AD

Gift of Julius Praeter

## "PIPTU WUHTI"
Hopi female caricature figure or clown

Cottonwood   3" x 11"
Arizona, USA, 20th C

Gift of Louise Padelford

## NAVAJO RUG

Wool   48" x 34"
Arizona, USA, 20th C

Gift of Mr. and Mrs. R. E. Hazard

POTTERY PLATE
Maria Martinez and son, Popovi Da

burnished earthenware, 6" d.
San Ildefonso Pueblo, New Mexico

Gift of C. Norman and Dorothy H. Hicks

ESKIMO AND BELUGA
A silkscreen print by Henry Napartuk

Paper  9" x 6"
Alaska, USA, 20th C

Gift of Anna Saulsbery

ᓇᐳ Henry Napartuk ᓱᐊᓇᖮ ᓇᐳ Eskimo and beluga.

ESKIMO DOLL

Caribou bone   1" x 3"
Alaska, USA, 20th C

Gift of Mrs. H. A. Still

WEATHERVANE

Metal   27" x 18"
USA, 19th C

154   Gift of Elizabeth Gordon

CARVED HORSE

painted wood, 4½' h.
Early American, 19th C

156    Museum purchase

Art dwells not only within culture and society, but also within every individual.

The Arts...reveal themselves all around us in the form of furniture, textiles, clothing, and other useful and decorative objects.

This view of life — culture — Art leads to the conclusion that there are no absolute boundaries between the most sophisticated art and folk art, crafts, and the manifestation of the individual in any detail of culture.

*Charmaine and Maurice Kaplan*

## Donors to Mingei International's Permanent Collection

Carolyn Allington
Come Fly A Kite / American Tin Cannery
Norman H. Anderson
Arara Enterprises, Mr. Claudio DeLuca
Judy Argyes
Ofelia Armer
Mrs. Joseph Aron
Richard C. and Mildred C. Atchinson
Barbara Baehr
Rosemary Baer
Dinesh A. Bahadur
Hallie Barcklay
Mrs. Jarvis Barlow
Elizabeth Bartlett
Mr. and Mrs. Robert E. Baumberger
Rocky Behr
Jane Bender
Andrew and Dorothy D. Benson
Steve Berger
Dr. Charles L. Bernier
Doreen Blumhardt
John Boehme
Dorothy Bolyard
A. W. Borsam
Barbara Bovee
John W. Boyd
Yvonne Courtenaye Brown
Anthony Brown
Mr. and Mrs. Bruce Brown
Mr. and Mrs. Anthony Browne
Betty and Robert Buffum
Mr. and Mrs. Edmund Burke,
    The Frank Papworth Estate
Mrs. Leon Campbell
Mr. and Mrs. Charles Cannon
The Carlsbad Library
Rhea Case
Dr. and Mrs. David Castner
Mrs. Robert Cate (Katarina Real)
Lois Chadwick
Gallery Eight
    courtesy of Mrs. Martin Chamberlain
Walter and Jane Chapman
Headmistress Kobai Naruse,
    Chiko School of Ikebana
China Books and Periodicals
    c/o Cathy McKeown
Mrs. William Colburn
Roger and Lisa Cole
Joanne Connelly
Marcella Cornish
Florence Covell

Arlene Cox
Robert Cugno
Mr. and Mrs. Benner Cummings
Mr. and Mrs. Robert Dahlgren
Nan Danninger
Mrs. Kirk J. David, Clare Jordan Estate
Susan Davis
Mrs. S. A. Davis
Paul W. and Esther M. Davis
Walter Deming
Dorothy Dixon
Norma Lundholm Djerassi
Mr. and Mrs. Robert Donnell
Euneva Dunn
Mr. and Mrs. Charles E. DuPont
Sue Earnest
Dr. Steven Emmet
Harry and Virginia Evans
Virginia Evans
Priscella D. Fawcett
Festival of India
Robert C. Fielding
Dr. and Mrs. Jonathan Fielding
Olga Fisch
Nancy Fitzwilliams
Virginia Flagg
Susan Fox
Lillian Frank
Elizabeth Freeman
Dr. Fay Frick
Gordon Frost
Mr. and Mrs. Richard A. Frost
Tonia Gale
Mr. and Mrs. Webster Gelman
Mr. and Mrs. Morse Gevanthor
The Golden Door
Ronald Goldenson, M.D.
Virginia Gale Gooch
Mr. and Mrs. John E. Goode
Elizabeth Gordon
Elfie Guillen
Sybille Haddock
Dorothy Haines
Dr. Raphael Hanson
Edwin T. and Elizabeth A.Harte
Leonard Hassan
Carmen Massip de Hawkins
Mr. and Mrs. R. E. Hazard, Jr.
Lola Heckelman
Steven A. Heller
Pricilla Henderson

## Donors to Mingei International's Permanent Collection

Mr. and Mrs. Norman Hicks
Lenita Hill
Mr. and Mrs. Richard Hiller
Mr. and Mrs. John C. Holt
Doris W. Holt
Dr. and Mrs. Patrick Houlihan
Brig Gen. Henry C. Huglin (Ret.)
Joyce Hundal
Viletta Hutchinson
Korean Cultural Services, L. A.
The Helen Hyden Trust,
  c/o Nellie Anderson
Lois J. Hyman
Edward Inskeep
The Institute Joaquim Nabuco de
  Pesquisas Socias
International Gallery,
  Stephen Ross, Director
Erna Isieb
Ikebana International S. D. Chapter
Marian Jenkins
Ethel Porter-Johnson
Dr. and Mrs. Ronald W. Jue (Naomi)
Dorothy M. Kaiser
Louisa Kassler
Isamu Kawaguchi
Maurice Kawashima
Sue Keller
Genevieve C. Kennedy
George Kent and Assoc.
Kikkoman Corporation
June King
Mr. and Mrs. Robert O. Kinsey
Phyllis Devereux Kircheff
Genevieve Koester
Lillian Kornblum
Frederick and Stella Krieger
H. Peter Krippl
General V. H. Krulak
Lillian Kuttnauer
Thornton Ladd
Evelyn Lakoff
Winnie Langley
Horton Larew
Bet Lawson
Mr. and Mrs. George Lazarnick
Mrs. J. Lebell
Molly Kao Lee
Wendy Lee
Mrs. B. Lesser
Ann Lindgren
Erik P. Lingren for Paul A. Lingren

Anna Marie Lininger
James C. Litz
Dr. and Mrs. Harvey Lobelson
Martha W. Longenecker
Will and Lana B. Lorenz
Warren Mackenzie
Betty MacNeill
Raye Malouff
Charlotte Mann
Michael Mansfield
Shirley Mariani
Alice Marquis
Margaret Martin
Slava Martin
Dolly Maw
Dr. Stefan Max
Keiko Mazza
Phila L. McDaniel
Mrs. W. B. McHugh
Ruth McHugh
Geraldine Murray McKay
Anne McMullin
Dr. Nilufer Medora
Elinor Meadows
Fred and Barbara Meiers
Dr. and Mrs. Arthur Metcalfe (Jeannette)
Mrs. Lyle Michael
Dorothy Miller
Justin Miller
Harriet Miller
Lily and Ana-Tole Minc
Shirley Miriani
Lusia Mitchell
Dr. Donald and Barbara Moore
Ann and Monroe Morgan
Moses
Mary Bryant Mosher
Mr. and Mrs. Glenn Murdock
Arihiko Natsume
Estate of Stanca Cella Neamtu,
  Stefan Bortnowski
Peter Nelson
Dr. Max Nelson
Mr. and Mrs. Nicholas Niciphor
Mr. and Mrs. Nicoloff
Calvert E. Norland
Mr. and Mrs. Corliss R. Nugent
Denni O'Bryan
Mr. and Mrs. Peter O'Reilly
Helenka Osborn
Judith Osgood
Dr. Louise H. Padelford

## Donors to Mingei International's Permanent Collection

Mr. and Mrs. Charles Padelford
Claire Paget
Mr. and Mrs. Edmund Burke
    for Frank Papsworth's Estate
Elizabeth Pascoe
Mrs. Theodore C. Paulson
Mr. and Mrs. John Payne
Mrs. Douglas J. Peacher
Marie Pearce
Mrs. M. A. Peele
Mr. Marshall and Ms. Hariett Peller
Sanford S. and Beverly P. Penner
Diane Pennington
Mrs. Lawrence Peterson
Mr. M. D. Philippe
Stephanie G. Phillips
Robert T. Pirazzini
Mr. and Mrs. James S. Plaut
Diane Powers
Julius Prater
Committee for the
    Preservation of Palestinian Heritage
Mrs. Hubert Price
Joanne Prigmore
Jordan Society / Queen Noor
Betty Rawitsch
Ellen Revelle
Beatrice E. Richardson
Seonaid Robertson
Anne Rohe
Martha W. Roth
Nasr Salem
San Diego Historical Society
San Diego Museum of Art
Hikaru Sasahara
Anna M. Saulsbery
Dr. and Mrs. H. Schwartz
Elizabeth L. Scott
Mrs. Gus Scurlock
Tom Sefton
Caroline Self
Hunton and Priscilla Sellman
Keisuke Serizawa
Anne Rohe for Ruth Adella Sessler
Homi and Nelly Sethna
Lee Shadell
Moshe and Lee Shapiro
Millard and Mary Sheets
Mrs. Thomas L. Shepherd (Ruth)
John Siglow
Dr. and Mrs. Clark Simm
Mr. and Mrs. Bill Simmons

Lucy Simpson
Esther and Morgan Sinclaire
Esther Sinclaire
Louette Smith
Bernard Smolin
    in memory of Mims Smolin
Jerry Stearnes
    in memory of Dorothy P. Sorensen
Mr. and Mrs. Fred A. Stebler
Connie Stengel
Mr. and Mrs. Worley W. Stewart
Mrs. H. A. Still
L. Keester Sweeney
Margaret H. Swenson
Evelyn Swift
Mr. and Mrs. Jean Swiggert
Deborah Szekely
Therese Tanalski
Mr. and Mrs. Horton R. Telford
Florence Temko
Shokensai Toko, Jr.
Mrs. Takahama Toshie
Tina Trejo
Mrs. Ross Treseder
Major John Van Buren
Mrs. William Vennard
Louise Venrick
Mitzie Verne
Stella Oeiding Warner
Robert Warwick
Elizabeth V. Watson
Julia K. Watson
Mr. and Mrs. William Watson
Mr. and Mrs. John Weaver
Douglas Webster
Mr. and Mrs. Christopher Weil
Howard Weinstein
Mrs. Samuel Weston
Mrs. W. Deykes Whitney
Col. and Mrs. Albert J. Wick
Mr. and Mrs. George F. Wick
Ginger Wideman
Mary Helen Williams
Sonnie Willis
Kent and Lana Wilson
Shirley Wimmer
Joyce Winkel
Nancy Winters
Mr. and Mrs. Charles M. Wood
Beatrice Wood
Shirley S. Wynne
Lydia Yancey

## Exhibitions Organized and Presented 1978–1993

- FOLK TOYS OF THE WORLD

- A CULTURAL MOSAIC – The Folk Arts of Brazil

  WEARABLE FOLK ART – Adaptations of Traditional Ethnic Garments

- RITES OF PASSAGE – Textiles of the Indonesian Archipelago from the Collection of Mary Hunt Kahlenberg

  MINGEI OF JAPAN – Known and Unknown

- KEISUKE SERIZAWA – A Living Treasure of Japan

  THE DENTZEL CAROUSEL TRADITION – Five Generations of an American Folk Art

  EARLY AMERICAN QUILTS AND WEATHERVANES – The Collection of Bill Pearson

  THE EYE OF THE TIGER – Folk Arts of Korea

- ¡ VIVAN LOS ARTESANOS ! – Mexican Folk Art from the Collection of Fred and Barbara Meiers

- INDIA – Village, Tribal Ritual Arts

- ROMANIAN FOLK ARTS – A Travelling Exhibition from the Bucharest Museum

- IKAT OF INDIA – Contemporary Weaves of Orissa and Andhra Pradesh

  TRAINS, DOLLS AND INTERNATIONAL FOLK TOYS

- LAURA ANDRESON – A Retrospective in Clay

- EVE GULICK – Three Decades of Weaves and Innovations

  A FEAST OF COLOR – Dance Costumes of Corpus Christi Festival of Ecuador

- IKAT WEAVES, BASTAR TRIBAL BRONZES AND MUSICAL INSTRUMENTS OF INDIA

- PATTERNS OF PARADISE – The Styles and Significance of Bark Cloth Around the World.

- TODOS SANTOS

- ETHIOPIA – Folk Art of a Hidden Empire

  THE ART OF TANTRA – A Cosmic Sign Language

  COUSINS AROUND THE WORLD – Photography of Norman Cousins

- SAMI DAIDDA – Art of Lapland

- THE HORSE SHOW

  MINGEI OF JAPAN

- PAPER INNOVATIONS – Cut, Folded and Molded Handmade Paper

- FORMS OF MOTHER EARTH – Contemporary Terracottas of India

  TWO HUNDRED AND TEN YEARS WITHOUT END – The Continuity of American Design from Colonial Times through the Work of Selected Contemporary Designers/Craftsmen.

  PUPPETRY OF CHINA

  DESIGNS FOR THE BODY – New Norwegian Jewelry

  THE BIRTH SYMBOL IN TRADITIONAL WOMEN'S ART – From Eurasia and the Western Pacific

MILLARD SHEETS' PAINTINGS – and Related Selections from his International Art Collection

FIRST COLLECTIONS – Dolls and Folk Toys of the World

ALL FLAGS FLYING – American Patriotic Quilts as Expressions of Liberty

MITHILA – IMAGES OF LIFE – Contemporary Ritual Paintings and Sculpture of Northern Bihar, India

INTERLACING – The Elemental Fabric – The Collection of Jack Lenor Larsen

A TRANSCULTURAL MOSAIC – Selections from the Permanent Collection of Mingei International

EARL CUNNINGHAM – His Carefree American World

LURES OF THE ICE – Fish Decoys from the Collection of William Bender

FOLK ART OF THE SOVIET UNION – Reflections of a Rich, Cultural Diversity of the Fifteen Republics

SPIRIT OF AMERICA – Early American and Contemporary Art of the People, By the People and For the People

MAYAN THREADS – Textile Art Treasures of the Ixchel Museum, Guatemala

FLORA AND FAUNA – Continuity of Plant and Animal Themes in Mesoamerican Art

TIBET – Art of the People from the Rooftop of the World

THE OTHER FACE – Indonesian Dance Masks and Related Art of Indonesia

OUT OF THE EAST – Palestinean Embroideries and Jewelry Reflecting Moslem, Christian and Jewish Traditions

ARROWS OF THE SPIRIT – Timeless Art Treasures of Native American Indians

CALLING ALL ANGELS – The First Annual Presentation of the Beatrice Richardson Angel Collection donated to Mingei International

FROM THE LAND OF THE SILK DRAGON – Textiles and Silver Adornment of Guizhou, China

MINGEI OF JAPAN – Living Traditions of Ceramics and Related Arts

HEIRLOOMS OF THE FUTURE – Masterworks of Living West Coast American Designers/Craftsmen

**Forthcoming**

TEMPLE CLOTHS, TERRACOTTAS AND ORNAMENTAL ARTS OF INDIA – From the Permanent Collection of Mingei International

KINDRED SPIRITS – Utility, Simplicity and Tranquility in American Shaker and Japanese Daily Art

Documentary exhibition publications.

**Corporate Associates**

THE HAHN COMPANY

**Director's Circle**

Chairmen
The HON. and MRS. ALBERT N. WILLIAMS

MR. and MRS. FRANK D. ALESSIO
MS. FRANCES ARMSTRONG
MR. and MRS. J. SAMUEL
  ARMSTRONG
MS. BARBARA BAEHR
DR. and MRS. JOHN J. BERGAN
MS. CAROLE A. BRANSON
MR. and MRS. ROY K. BLACK
MS. BETTY U. BUFFUM
MR. and MRS. HUGH CARTER
MR. and MRS. DALLAS CLARK
MR. DAVID COPLEY
DR. ROGER C. CORNELL
DR. SUSAN CRUTCHFIELD
MR. and MRS. MARC H. CUMMINGS
MR. and MRS. ALEX DeBAKCSY
MR. and MRS. HARRY DeHAAN
MR. and MRS. MICHAEL DESSENT
DR. and MRS. CHARLES C. EDWARDS
MR. and MRS. J. L. FRITZENKOTTER
AUDREY GEISEL
MR. and MRS. JOHN GILCHRIST
MR. and MRS. JOHN GOODE
DR. and MRS. HUGH GREENWAY
MRS. ERNEST W. HAHN
MS. JUDITH HARRIS and
  DR. ROBERT SINGER
MR. WILLIAM M. HAWKINS, JR.
MR. and MRS. BRUCE HEAP
MR. WILLIAM E. HEYLER
MRS. JOAN HOLTER
MR. and MRS. KEVIN D. HOYLE
ALAN and NORA JAFFE
MR. and MRS. MAURICE KAPLAN
MRS. LOUISA KASSLER
MR. MAURICE M. KAWASHIMA
MR. and MRS. JAMES KERR
MRS. HELEN W. KORMAN
MR. ARMAND LABBE
DR. and MRS. DON LEIFFER
MRS. NANCY LEONARD

MR. and MRS. GEORGE M. PARDEE
DR. and MRS. S. S. PENNER
DIANE POWERS
MR. DALE REIS
MR. and MRS. GEORGE RODES
RADM and MRS. W. HALEY ROGERS
MRS. MARTHA W. ROTH
MRS. RUTH F. SHEPHERD
MR. BRADLEY SMITH
MR. and MRS. WORLEY W. STEWART
MRS. WALTER SWANSON
MR. and MRS. THEODORE T. TANALSKI
MR. and MRS. HORTON TELFORD
MR. and MRS. JOHN M. THORNTON
DR. and MRS. HAROLD K. TICHO
MRS. BARBARA WALBRIDGE
MR. and MRS. FRANK WARREN
MR. and MRS. HAROLD B. WILLIAMS
MR. and MRS. WALTER J. ZABLE

**Patrons**

DR. BERNARD W. AGINSKY
MRS. WILLOUGHBY BISHOP
DR. and MRS. KIRK DAVID
MRS. CAROLYN FARRIS
MRS. MERIE DAVIS
MR. and MRS. KENNETH V. HILL
MRS. MADELINE L. GOLDBERG
DR. STEFAN MAX
MR. and MRS. RAY MUZQUIZ
THE PRICE FAMILY FUND
MRS. ELLEN REVELLE
MARIE MURPHY-SINGER and
  DAVID R. SINGER

166

## Major Sponsors 1978–1993

### Individuals

Margaret Barlow
J. Dallas and Mary H. Clark
Norma Djerassi
Audrey S. Geisel
Sidney and Eve Gulick
Jean and Ernest Hahn
Alan and Nora Jaffe
Charmaine and Maurice Kaplan
Sydney Martin Roth
Anna M. Saulsbery
Millard and Mary Sheets
Mr. and Mrs. Worley W. Stewart
Rosemary Braun Utecht

### Foundations

Ahmanson Foundation
R. C. Baker Foundation
Legler Benbough Foundation
The Seymour E. Clonick Memorial Fund
The James S. Copley Foundation
The Nathan Cummings Foundation
The Drown Foundation
The Favrot Fund
The James Irvine Foundation
The Kerr Foundation
The Knight Aid Fund
Las Patronas
The Gerald and Inez Grant Parker
    Foundation
The Robert Peterson Foundation
The Roth Fund
The San Diego Community Foundation
Dr. Seuss Foundation
The Skaggs Foundation
Lila Wallace–Reader's Digest Fund
Weingart Foundation

### Corporations

Allen, Matkins, Leck, Gamble & Mallory
Bazaar del Mundo
California First Bank
Catellus Development Corporation
The Fluor Corporation
Ernest W. Hahn and University Towne
    Centre Associates
The Hahn Company
JMB Realty

Mervyn's
San Diego Gas and Electric

### Government Agencies

California Arts Council
The City of San Diego
The County of San Diego
Institute of Museum Services
The National Endowment for the Arts

**Museum Staff**

MARTHA W. LONGENECKER – Director
JAMES R. PAHL – Deputy Director
CAROL Z. KLICH – Executive Secretary
CHRISTINA L. ROJAS – Registrar
ROBERT B. SIDNER – Membership/Public Relations
DOROTHEA CRONOGUE – Publicist
BRYAN J. LOYCE – Security Guard
RESHMA J. SOLBACH – Mgr., Collector's Gallery
ANN V. PEDICORD – Assistant, Collector's Gallery

**Volunteer Staff**

NANCY J. ANDREWS – Librarian
VIRGINIA PANTONE – Volunteer Coordinator
EILEEN MILLER – Coordinator-Receptions
V'ANN CORNELIUS – Docent Coordinator
SUSAN EYER – Mailing Coordinator

**A Transcultural Mosaic**

DESIGN AND EDITING – Martha W. Longenecker
PHOTOGRAPHY – Lynton Gardiner   (except as noted)
TYPESETTING – Dee Kahler, Moog and Associates, Inc.
PRODUCTION ASSISTANT – Reshma J. Solbach
PRODUCTION FACILITATOR – Victor Arreola
PRINTING – Korea – Overseas Printing Co.

MINGEI INTERNATIONAL, a non-profit, public foundation is supported by memberships, volunteer services and tax deductible donations. Membership is open to all those interested in furthering the understanding of world folk art.

MINGEI INTERNATIONAL is accredited by the American Association of Museums. For information, please telephone: (619) 453-5300.